Just Passing Through

by

Mick Yates

First published 2022 by The Hedgehog Poetry Press

Published in the UK by
The Hedgehog Poetry Press
5, Coppack House
Churchill Avenue
Clevedon
BS21 6QW

www.hedgehogpress.co.uk

ISBN: 978-1-913499-81-5

A CIP Catalogue record for this book is available from the
British Library.

For my grandchildren

Maisie, Alice, Amelie,

Alyssa, Aiden, Ada

All of whom I hope will travel far in life

All of the poems in this collection

were written in the following nine cities

when I was just passing through

London, Nottingham, Leicester,

Cairo, Luxor, New York,

Stockholm, Bratislava, Budapest.

Contents

'We are all visitors to this time, this place

We are all just passing through

Our purpose here is to observe, to learn, to grow, to love

And then we return home'

An Australian Aboriginal Proverb

nine cities of the world

it is good to sit out

on summer nights in any city

eating good food

drinking fine wine and coffee

watching the world go by

feeling the pulse of life

the endless movement of existence

it helps a person to feel

connected and solitary at the same time

emulating heroes

in search of his inspiration

wordsworth favoured long walks in the country with dorothy

whereas coleridge preferred a drop or two of laudanum for company

and baudelaire a tipple of absinthe with an opium chaser

rimbaud liked the booze mostly and occasional hashish

plus recreational gun-running in between

ginsberg kerouac and the other beat poets

favoured a spliff or two of marijuana

or dropping the odd tab of acid

those wild boys byron and shelley

hell they tried it all and more

that no good boyo dylan thomas

liked copious beer and whisky chasers see

not to mention the grand excesses of bukowski

it can really be quite good fun

standing on the shoulders of giants

waiting for the muse to arrive

for inspiration to finally set me free

the night

the night

has its own sounds

its own kind of music

if you take time to listen

the night is its own day

it has its own brightness

though the sun no longer shines

the stars do sometimes

the night is a place of rebirth

of other beginnings in life

it is the end of what has gone

and the start of something new

staking my claim

since i emerged into this world

and for as long as i can remember

i have mined life for its hidden secrets

i have taken a pick and shovel

and set to work diligently every day

so far however i have found

nothing of significance yet

no nuggets of wisdom

no seam of understanding to call my own

i catch my reflection in the mirror

as the evening sun slowly sets

touch the wiry stubble on my chin

see my wrinkled skin scarred with time

and smile at myself and who i have become

knowing the secret lode

is still out there somewhere

waiting to be found

war veteran

there was an article in a national newspaper

he died shortly before the end of last year

on the cold streets of a city somewhere

he had post-traumatic stress disorder

he was homeless he was cold

neither was he very old

still a relatively young man

who was sleeping rough

his reward for serving his country well

on tours of active duty in the army

he was mostly ignored by all who passed him by

unknown unseen and unimportant

gone now though he may be

he is not forgotten at least by me

rest with dignity

rest in peace

hero

a romantic tale

our house

is like wuthering heights

it is a house that is designed

to compete with the very worst weather

that only the most brutal winters here can give

so live here awhile

be my cathy

and after we are long gone

they will sing our song

of the worst that winter has to give

and of what it was once to live

and to love

and to smile

faux pas

i have seen that look from you

so many times before

and i know what it means

that i have drunk far too much alcohol for sure

or maybe i also said something

rather inappropriate once more?

what have i done? what dreadful social gaffe

have i committed this time?

although quite honestly what does it matter anyway?

yet another construct of civilised society

where the codes of conduct are understood

and any kind of deviation from the norm

is regarded as a form of heresy and punished accordingly

with total social exclusion for failing to conform

and what is more i shall be banished from the golf club door

and my mere presence at the masonic lodge tonight

will be scrutinised further i am sure

sabotage

the sound of a radio

either transistor or digital

is an important part of my life

in most of the rooms of our home

i have a radio playing

quietly almost subliminally

in the background

in the kitchen it is radio two

in the study classic fm

in the front bedroom radio four

in the lounge smooth fm

and in the bathroom radio three

when i am not alone in the house

someone goes round the rooms

switching these radio stations off

while i return slightly later

to turn them all on again

i suspect it is my wife my partner in life

i have not caught her red-handed yet

but it is only a matter of patience

and of time

a morbid preoccupation

my wife thinks it is odd

that i should record the deaths

of my family and close friends

in my personal journal

my aunt did that also as i recollect

in a large black family bible

and i suppose it is in my genes also

it is not macabre or strange to me

i am merely acknowledging the lives of those

who were important and precious to me

i am simply putting the final pieces

into the jigsaw puzzle of our existence

and the finishing touches

to the canvas of my life

a bravura performance

(in memory of my mother who suffered from alzheimer's)

the face that you portray to the world

is a clever construct a cunning disguise

a jekyll and hyde façade

however if i told your loyal audience

what i believe and think i know

nobody would understand me though

on the stage of life you are the consummate actor

ever the professional you play your part so well

for they do not understand the mask you wear

and will never see you as i do

until the mask slips eventually

and you forget your lines publicly

or are slow in your delivery

only when the mask is finally gone

will you then stand centre stage alone

naked stripped bare forever

calling for a prompt

that will never come

neighbour

martin aged forty four

lives with his mother in the house next door

he has never been married he has never had a girlfriend

in the eleven years i have been here

he has done the same driving job

for the past twenty years or more

off at six in the morning

back at six for his tea

after driving halfway round the country

he has passed through many places

in his solitary career but leaves no trace behind

he never goes out he has no friends

he exists as a virtual recluse

he spends no money from his wages

he must be an eccentric millionaire

he says hello only if prompted

he can sometimes manage goodbye

though he never seems quite sure why

am i missing something here?

i mean is that really the way

that you would like to live then die?

travelling light

packing it all together to go

takes me all of fifteen minutes

it has always been so in my life

there have been so many partings

so many leavings along the way

my bag has always been open

waiting in anticipation for the day

when the lure of a new future

beckons me once more

and i walk out yet again

through an ever open door

nostalgia

my dear sister we have talked so often

about returning there just you and me

of travelling back across the irish sea

to the small beautiful isle of man

where we once spent so many holidays

in a much different and more golden time

when we were both young children

and the days seemed always hot and sunny

the beach full of our sandcastles but otherwise empty

the sea was deep blue and the cottage in the harbour cosy

the scenery varied and spectacular the cream teas simply yummy

is it wise though ever to go back to where you once were happy?

for the past can never be reconstructed exactly

or as ideally as it was back then

since nothing can ever be the same again

times have moved on things have changed

and will never be again i am sure

as they were once upon a time before

there is simply no point in going back

to search in vain for something

that is not there anymore

a short visit

for the last three days

i have holidayed in hell

and its name was cairo

but the desert sands the pyramids

and the antiquities of the museum

are way beyond comparison

almost heavenly in themselves

alienation

loneliness is worse

in a big city

it bites more viciously

into the heart and soul

leaving anxious thoughts

in the darkest hours

of the night

conversing with bees

it is a hot summer day

i am sitting in the garden

in one of my uncertain moods

considering the imponderables of existence

like what is the meaning of life?

whilst searching for answers

i watch the honey bees at work

hovering from flower to flower

humming happily as they go about their business

what is the meaning of life? i enquire of them

we are not really bothered much

about the imponderables of existence they answer

we are merely bees moving from flower to flower

seeking out the sweet nectar of life

miracles

the world we live in

is not always the logical place

we mostly believe it to be

for beneath the surface of reality

there is another realm of magic and mystery

some long lost alchemy

we have still not learnt

how to harness effectively

look inwards as well as outwards

for some explanation some sign

of what there is we have yet to find

in these other recesses of the mind

for the cosmos is unique in its design

and only if you believe in miracles

will one ever come your way

i ching

you are the book of changes

so tell me something new

give me words of wisdom

in this time of drought

i have thrown the coins

i have read the text

so tell me now please

what is coming next?

you are the great oracle

and only you know the score

so tell me what the future holds

i need to know some more

tell me what things lie in store

show me what kind of future lies ahead

do i keep on living?

or am i better off dead?

apocalypse

last night there was a wild storm

the wildest i have ever known

lightning ravaged the sky

like a crowd of dragons arguing

spitting fire across the blackness

singeing the world below

then came the profane language

of the venomous thunder

swearing at me for being merely mortal

and not entirely innocent anymore

soon to be closely followed by the rain

a deluge almost biblical in proportion

maybe the heavens are truly angry

with their wayward flawed creation?

tapestry

you are all of the threads

in the rich and colourful

tapestry of my life

you are woven so deeply

in my heart and soul

i think i might unravel

without you by my side

whoever crafted so well

our affection for each other

is a supreme weaver

of dreams and of love

a slow thaw

why am I so cold?

because six of your
close friends and relatives
have died in this one year

will I ever get warmer?

it will get warmer in time
but a chill in your heart
will always remain

why must it be like this?

because your love for them
burned brightly as a fire
and now only embers remain

resurrection

the long cold months of winter

are at last finally vanishing

and the dead dark time

has now given way to spring

buds appear on the trees

flowers thrust their green shoots

up towards heaven once more

do not doubt the concept of rebirth

for the evidence of a new life

lies all around you everywhere

if you care to look and believe

and death shall hold no power

in this realm of everlasting life

the river flows

it starts high in the mountains

as a small trickle nothing more

full of life and energy

gaining confidence and power

as it grows in size and volume

ever onwards it flows

broadening on the flat plains

in the middle stretches of its journey

solid and certain of its way

in its later stages

it reaches full maturity as it nears the sea

beyond the golden strand

there lies a vast ocean

full of hope and mystery

i will meet you there some day

let me count the ways

how do i love you?

why in so many ways

it would take forever

to count them all

you will have to make do therefore

with the very few i can offer you

during the brief time

that we can spend together

in this glorious world

so let us take the best we have got

stash them in a small backpack

and walk through life together

exploring the many other ways

before our time runs out forever

terra incognita

i do not know this land

i have not travelled here before

i am a stranger alone

curious to see what i shall find

sad for what i will leave behind

questions and answers

do you take pleasure in this world?

for all its faults it is a place
still full of wonder

do you understand why you are here?

not really but i go with the flow
and keep on searching for some meaning

do you have someone you love?

there are many people i love

then you are a very fortunate person
and very close to discovering the secret

does that make you happy?
it makes me very happy

poems

after all

they are only small bundles

of words tied together with string

sometimes containing a meaning

but more often filled with emotion

the sorts of feelings

we all experience sometimes

in our individual lives

things that you may recognise

like the message in a bottle

a castaway might find

that gets washed up one day

on the shore of a desert island

somewhere long ago and far away

carpe diem

this is it

this and nothing more

this brief span is all you get

so make every minute count

the light will shine sometimes

even in your darkest hours

you will get your share of chances

be sure to seize them when they come

make the most of them you can

be constantly on the lookout

for fun and frivolity in your life

and keep tough for the hard times

you can never escape the grim reaper

but you can still evade him sometimes

keep ducking and diving always

make him work hard my friend

strive always in your life

to be the best you can be

you are splendid in your creation

the gods know it

and will make you welcome one day

feeling my age

i am getting old

i know i am

i am getting old

because i still want

to talk to real people

over dinner in a restaurant

instead of watching them stare

at the screens of their mobile phones

i prefer human communication

and sensory interaction

to staring at an electronic machine

whatever happened to the art of conversation?

sanctuary

there has always

been a space inside me

whenever my life has become hard

and my prospects slim

a quiet oasis where i can hide

lick my wounds

and prepare for whatever

the future might bring

in this place of refuge

personal failure has no relevance

neither does it carry any stigma

the only important thing

is simply how well

you walk through the wreckage

the joy of simple things

smart phones and smart computers

smart televisions and smart washing machines

and all the other smart electronic devices we rely on

why are they all so complex these days?

why are they all so difficult to use?

why are they always trying to think for me?

to predict what they anticipate it is i want?

it has nothing to do with my age

i would still have felt the same when i was younger

life is meant to be simple like my old transistor radio

that works on two small batteries and goes on forever

like my simple handheld corkscrew bottle opener

to open my red wine or my bottles of beer

like turning the pages of a real book

that you can see and touch and smell

and hear and even taste

as you read it late at night

by warm and soothing candlelight

the vanishing point

in the warm light

from the kitchen window

two white lines radiate out of sight

from the walls of our home

our washing lines taut in the darkness

devoid of clothes and late at night

stretch out in the distance

to the point where they meet

on the wall of the outside shed

where they join up eventually

is this the end of all things in life?

an unseen point in the blackness?

an absence of visible light?

or maybe just the beginning of something else?

nighthawks

sometimes on train journeys late at night

i look through the windows

of the houses as they pass by

peering through the open curtains of strangers

trying to see who is living there

wondering what jobs they do

whether they are happy or sad

sometimes i catch a glimpse into their nocturnal world

and realise they are very much like me

all doing mostly the same ordinary things

yet constantly on the lookout for some hopeful sign

always searching for some deeper meaning

for some greater purpose in life

trying to make some sense of it all

trying to create order from the chaos

unlike the artist edward hopper though

i do not paint what i see through the windows

on train journeys late at night

although sometimes the next morning

i do try to write it down on paper

vernal

the world is unfolding in new ways

the sap is rising again for sure

leaves are spreading in the warm sun

tight buds bursting open for the sheer fun

of leaving winter far behind them

blood flows in the veins of lovers again

sweet words are whispered in the ears of spring

witness this spectacle throw open the door

enjoy the beginning of everything once more

travellers

never really here

never really there

never really anywhere

any place is as good as another

any lover who comes along

who sings the same song

is one worth waiting for

for as long as it lasts or never

wake up in the morning

early when the air is clear

smell which way to steer

get it right and sail along

steer the whole day long

see where the journey takes you

feel what it makes you

sometimes calm seas sometimes never

see where it takes you my friend

whatever the weather

follow it to the end

forever in eden

i moved here
quite late in life
to start again

it was a saturday
when i first passed
this way
into eden
met a local lass
by chance
at a mayday dance
and was lost in love

like the gypsies
that come roaming by
we walk the valley
we climb the hill
fish the stream
and dream
such dreams
of new horizons

in the summer fine
we drink wine
in the winter chill
sloe gin

it is a good
place to begin

maybe i will
stay here
some time

speculation

who are we you and me?

two travellers each on a separate journey?

or two star-crossed lovers maybe

estranged by geography and destiny?

two hearts two minds two souls

snagged in a tangled web of circumstance

none of which is of our own design

one day when the tides of life

set us free from our ties that bind

we may travel together as one

united at last in body and mind

exploring the roads we have yet to travel

holding hands sharing a common destination

the name of which let us call romance

maybe someday we two may become one

free as we were intended to be

so tell me would you take the chance

if that day were ever to come?

About Mick Yates

Mick Yates lives in the far north of England. He has worked extensively as a playwright and has had more than thirty plays produced at theatres across the country. He has received many awards including an Edinburgh Festival Fringe First and The Benn Levy Award. He has also written for television, most notably for the BBC series *Doctors*. His debut poetry collection *artefacts* won the 2014 Geoff Stevens Memorial Poetry Prize and was published by Indigo Dreams Publishing in 2015. His second collection *kaleidoscope* was published by them in 2017. *the art of conversation* was published by the New York based Clare Songbirds Publishing House in 2018.

Another collection *the shapes of passion* was also published by Clare Songbirds Publishing House in 2018 to be followed by *random thoughts from the north* which was published by them in 2019. His next collection *the blue hour* was published by The Hedgehog Poetry Press in 2019. He was longlisted in 2017, 2018 and 2019 for Best Poetry Pamphlet in the prestigious Saboteur Awards and was also a Pushcart Prize nominee in 2018. His pamphlet *poems from egypt* was published by Barley Cottage Publications in 2020 and five other pamphlets *forever in eden , conversing with bees, a river flows through here, from the fells to the sea,* and *bittersweet* were also published by them in 2020.

Ingram Content Group UK Ltd.
Milton Keynes UK
UKHW040724080323
418175UK00004B/447